Weaker than Water

Katherine Gotthardt

Weaker than Water

Katherine Gotthardt

Second Edition
Copyright KMG Publishing, 2016

First Edition Published 2013

This publication is also available as an e-book through Amazon Digital Services, Inc. ASIN: B00C6P5NW2

In the world, there is nothing more submissive and weak than water.
Yet for attacking that which is hard and strong, nothing can surpass it.
–Lao Tzu

Contents

Dedication

For my family and friends, as well as for those
in the community
—both physical and virtual—
who have inspired and encouraged me.
You are my angels, and I hope you know who
you are

.

About Abundance

Unbury the life you once had,
the one you'd long forgotten,
the one before the stars were born.

Unbury the life you wish to live,
the marvel of superb minnows,
of ivy and turtles and silence,
and the surprise that released you
the first time you recognized

you were never made
of manure and mud,
but of sun and rain and angels,
feeding you with fingers
of abundance.

My God Rides the Metro

My God rides the Metro.
He watches tunnels blur by
like ages prodded en windowed route,
sudden stops of thought.

He smiles at soft-fingered children
kneeling on orange benches,
eyes and noses conceiving steam
on this miraculous glass.

My God rides the Metro.
He holds his breath as it climbs,
skips in its tracks into sunlight,
plods over passing waters,

those unknowing rowers below.
God smells hard work and damp papers,
notices holes in briefcases and bags,
watches for auras most of us miss
as we wish for the stop at our station.

My God rides the Metro,
but no one ever looks up.
He sighs alongside travelers,
crowds with perspiring eyes.

God sees himself in passengers,
hopes we might seat ourselves near him,
or nod in his general direction,
assure him he's still alive.

Prayer Remembered

At ten years old,
I tried laying
on of hands,
until I could no longer
suspend them above
your sleeping self.
I did not want you
to go to hell.
Not once did I ever touch you.

Recognition

I'm
not I
am who am.

Thank God!

Meek
and poor
are blessed? Whew!

Taking the Bullet

I
know my
value. Do you?

Tell
me, what
are your values?

Would
you die
for me, too?

In dependence

Please
understand. Your
love is desperation.

My
love is
somewhere with God.

You
mistake me
for salvation. Don't.

On the Inside Track

There is only
one sunny
spot,

where stands an
Asian man,
seeing

cherry blossoms in
winter. I'm
sure

of it, because
he shines
like

my most profound
moments, aged
wisdom,

or a kind
of benevolent
God.

Sanctuary

Elephants
are the
Buddha reincarnated. All
are worth
preserving.

The Book Under my Desk

Upside-down lotus flower,
pouring pink from leaf to petal-tip;
all I can see is part of the title:
Idiot's Guide to Buddhism.

Buddha Untitled

My little silver Buddha,
meditating on my monitor,
his base reflected in black,
the folds of his robe tarnished.

Año de Muerto

aquí
must be
the death year.

gracias
por todos,
everything I love.

solicitud:
be my
backyard perennial flower?

Cure

Do not silence
your life.
Disregard
fears of tonsillitis,
laryngitis, infection.
Sing.

Sing what is,
what was,
what
isn't. Trill your
years. Match
pitch

with decades, tone
with seasons.
Entice
octaves with each
drink of ice
water,
followed by spoons
of soup.
Sip.

Hear how clear
your truth
sounds?

Niagara

Sometimes my story
crashes like sorrow, water
dumped high from the falls.

Milkweed

Grey milkweed on my desk,
husk like a tough survivor,
pillar of seeds dried inside,
already ready for spring.

Prayer

Today's requisition:
water for calmness
under fire.

Realistically Speaking

I've no desire
to reach
sainthood,

or beatifiedhood or
perfecthood or
blamelesshood,

Godhood, famoushood, allnicenesshood,
saviorhood, Allahood,
Buddhahood.

I just want
to be
good.

You Looked Like My Brother

One day, I taught agape,
another, love thy neighbor,
brotherly love like Christians.
I should have known by your eyes.

Stick to the topic, Katherine.
You're not even really Christian.
And you certainly ain't no preacher.

Grotto

Sometimes a storm strips my mind
down to a puff, a bird's
cry for mercy and worms.

And I, in my now naked head,
wander back to the monastery,
the grotto, the place my parents brought me

when I was young. God was always a cloud,
beams streaming through gray,
like my most brilliant self.

The Convincing

Surely the way you wove that last path proves
to the deities you could have made us
in seven days or less! That filial

yellow leaf, autumn splash on our earth, red
eyed Lord of maple trees and eccentric
vines, do they not argue in favor of
a Brahma, an Allah, or Great Spirit?

Come idols, admit you've made an error!
The folly is not in confessing; it's
denying this deluge of tree-babies

crawling the way for us, one tenuous
knee after another, green infant to
crimson teen to golden adult, leading
onward, knowing the others will follow.

My Third Eye Cried

My third eye cried
when I saw you try
to sell your own.

Prayer for Prisoners
at Christmas

Sirens are for those
who need saving. Coyotes'
songs are starved and sad.

I Saw God in the Elevator

I saw God in the elevator–
he looked like Morgan Freeman.
He wore an orange jumpsuit,
destination: cell block three.
I wondered what he was doing there,
and then I thought, of course.
He's headed for the top floor,
rising toward redemption.

Calling for Peace

Peace has white
wings, and only comes when you
call it. But you
have to know the right
names, those syllables you
have a hard time with. You
stumble over them like
a drunk in daylight,
and they, creatures of night.

*The body of 13-year-old Alexis "Lexie" Glover was
found Friday 1/9/2009 in a shallow creek near
McCoart Administration Building (Prince William
County, VA), two days after she went missing. Alexis
had sickle cell anemia and post-traumatic stress
disorder as well as autism. Alexis was adopted when
she was six. Her mother was found guilty of murder.*

For Alexis

One needn't know the river
to know the way it flows–
that is the way the Buddha knew
beneath the Bodhi tree.
He, emptying his mind into water,
washing his thoughts away,
came to understand an afterlife:

The feather becoming the fawn,
Banyan tree lighting the dawn,
immortality of everyone's energy,
the no-banks-needed mind.
The shell of every walnut
rises up to drink, while parching
Orchid tongues finally are wetted.

Speaking in the language of trickles–
that is how it is
even for the smallest stream:
flowing, rising, flowing,
then weeping one more time,
go peaceful little girl,
into ocean again.

Ode to a Balloon Let Go in London

It's what happens when an orb flies freely,
escaping the glass of a world glaring
with human imperfection, industry, idols,
what passes for intelligence and integrity–
it oversees London, the iris of England's
art, the reputation of queens, the relaxed
accent of ancient history revered or scorned
or adored. A balloon–

now there is something worth seeing,
air encouraging flight the second a grip
on the string loosens or a knot becomes undone
or our natural fascination with release
makes us raise our sights to a sun
running from tower top to tower top,

the oft referenced wandering cloud
wondering at the inscrutable irony
of rubber expecting its own explosion–no,
welcoming it, celebrating it, while ascending like a
soul, past its own reflection,
past the tired eye of Big Ben,
into the loving arms of infinity.

The Process

This is how
family is
made:
the ones closest
to sky
collecting
all that is
good in
the
rain, preserving it
in aqua
pura,

then pausing, then
dripping beauty
into
the mouths of
their young,
birds
with open beaks.
What they
can't
finish, they release
generously, gladly,
feeding
the rest of
a starving
world.

The Early Child

Were you perfect would I love you less?
I eye your ear, supple question mark,
but a mass where the dot should be, streak of scar
beneath the lobe where surgery takes it tax—
it seems monthly now—those horrific visits for
healing, clinically completing what my womb would
not, always a nightie and needle for forcing your sleep.

I have learned to look after each procedure,
worked at cementing my eyes to yours
even when bloody bandages prevent our
physical bond. My thoughts are always somewhere
on you—your head or mind or heart, and I wonder
what will be left when finally you heal?

Speaking of Earth

My children speak of the Earth
in the language of hopelessness:
"No one will do anything anyway."
"We should all ride horses,
replace cars. But no one listens."
"Wal-mart says they only use eco-friendly
products. But their light bulbs aren't."
"We don't need any more houses.
Why can't they just stop building?"

Mangy magazine pages and bread bags
claim our bony trees, last year's
Robin's eggs decay,
a deck peels five years of paint,
windows need replacing.
My children's retro music
condenses on the glass:
"Oh we're never gonna survive."

By Placid Bay
for my mother-in-law on the morning of her passing

These leaves,
white with winter,
and those frozen, spiky pine cones,
then, a cement barrier,
marked "no trespassing,"
protecting a broken dam–
seagulls pay no mind to signs.

On the side of the rough road,
two frozen dandelions, still yellow,
look ridiculously optimistic,
as a horn beeps off a hoard of vultures
blocking the street. They retreat,
return, my Australian Shepherd mix,
on a long, long leash,
gleefully chasing them away.

Reminders

The sun also
rises, my
child.

Every
season turns
on its heel.

Sunday Comfort

Reminding
myself, everything
will be okay.
I
carry no
painful sentence alone.

Gratitude

Gratitude
is why
I stayed alive.

Victory

Getting
up still
wins first prize.

Exceeding the Grasp

No
fingers left,
you reached
for me.

Time Keeping

My
wrist, punctured
by a watch.

A Spot of Tea

Instant
coffee, tea,
absolutely, not me.

You
need sugar,
cream, not me.

Scald
yourself with
water, not me.

Ad

I
posted, "Abusers
need not apply."

Someone Saw the Rabbit

Alice's
rabbit rushes
us to anxiety.

Medication

These
pills. The
look you give.

Request

Remember me. I
am not
free.

This for That

If sleep were
pills, I'd
OD.

If food was
drugs, I
did.

Sunday Outing

She had white pustules
packed tightly atop
knots of red, foundations
for infection, overwhelming
as city streets,
running from forehead

to fingertip. Her hair
was colorless brown,
cut with stolen scissors,
layers blunt, obvious as agony.
She reached out to touch my arm.
 "Don't do that," I said.
"I've already had it."

I pulled away,
felt my own cheek,
showed her the skin
on my hands, my wrists,
those soft places smoothed
by toil and miracle, by continuous
treatment and care.

"I can't let it come back," I said.
I folded my hands in front of me,
made my way down the theater aisle,
edges beaded in light,
guiding me to plush red seats
where my family sat,
waiting for the play to begin.

What It Does

More than anything,
I cry for freedom–
more than for white
frosting or dark chocolate,
money or a task-driven
nature. More than
for antidepressants,
anxiety medication
and pain pills, even
more than for feeling
a milkweed bursting
with gossamer and the sticky
stuff that connects fingers
to a fine, physical world
whispering, "Feel me."

I think it was the mandatory
hand washing that did it,
the hose that marked
my ungluing, water
pressure propelling me,
uprooted, ungrounded,
separated from even one
stray seed stuck to a sweater cuff,
me, spurted into a void
of metal and mixed messages.

They clank the jail doors
shut. "Let's see you
get out of this one," they gloat.

Being a Tree

varicose bark veins,
the tree's bald spot,
fingers wrinkled
in oaken shade,
splinters of a hundred
years–the fire,
the automobile, the war–
the semi-permeable
scent of smoke,
brown skin, white
skin, burnt skin,
some seasons
companion grasses
growing, sometimes left,
sometimes mowed. dew
droppings, bird showers
the indignity of summer
squirrels chuckling
at your age.
Is it so hard
to be a tree?

threat of ax, curse
of being born wood,
and always whispers
of uncertain storms,
you bend your branches,
slice your own trunk,
count your rings, waiting
to come back home.

About the Ending

It's all about the ending,
how the thing turns out,
how it lowers itself to the sidewalk
and sits, permanent as history,
a three-ton Buddha in the middle
of Central Square.

I detest unhappy endings,
even more so, meaningless ones,
so I make up my own.

This hurting creature heals
with help from terrorists-
turned-heroes, that poor village
restored by ironic justice.
Three lost climbers find direction
from the sun, the children's dog
was only in the bushes, and a heart,
reconstructed, pulses
on the once-dead monitor.

You're cured, ma'am.
You can go home now.

Hurt's Final Destination

Hurt
is only
a badly torn
skirt:

resolve to
throw it away.

Knot
the trash bag,
leave it
on the curb.

Allow the pros
to take it
somewhere to decompose.

About the Author

Katherine Mercurio Gotthardt is a poetry and prose writer residing in Western Prince William County, Virginia, where she enjoys exploring history, art, culture and nature. An advocate for preservation, conservation, education and civic engagement, Katherine volunteers for several non-profit organizations. A former freelance, community writer for the regional *News & Messenger* newspaper, Katherine has taught college English composition online and English as a Second Language (ESL) at an adult detention center. In January of 2014, Katherine founded All Things Writing, LLC, a full-service writing company.

Katherine has published three other books: *Poems from the Battlefield*, a collection of Civil War themed poetry, photos and period quotes; *Furbily-Furld Takes on the World*, an illustrated, children's epic poem; and *Approaching Felonias Park*, a novel focusing on themes in predatory lending.

For contact information, visit:
WWW.AllThingsWritingLLC.com

www.ingramcontent.com/pod-product-compliance
Lightning Source LLC
Chambersburg PA
CBHW071755020426
42331CB00008B/2312